My Favorite

I LOVE BASEBALL

By Ryan Nagelhout

Gareth Stevens
PUBLISHING

Please visit our website, www.garethstevens.com. For a free color catalog of all our high-quality books, call toll free 1-800-542-2595 or fax 1-877-542-2596.

Library of Congress Cataloging-in-Publication Data

Nagelhout, Ryan.
I love baseball / by Ryan Nagelhout.
p. cm. — (My favorite sports)
Includes index.
ISBN 978-1-4824-0720-4 (pbk.)
ISBN 978-1-4824-0767-9 (6-pack)
ISBN 978-1-4824-0719-8 (library binding)
1. Baseball — Juvenile literature. I. Nagelhout, Ryan. II. Title.
GV867.5 N34 2015
796.357—d23

First Edition

Published in 2015 by
Gareth Stevens Publishing
111 East 14th Street, Suite 349
New York, NY 10003

Editor: Ryan Nagelhout
Designer: Nick Domiano

Photo credits: Cover, p. 1 Zoran Milich/Allsport Concepts/Getty Images; pp. 5, 19, 24 (base, bat) Stockbyte/Thinkstock.com; p. 7 MikeC123/Shutterstock.com; p. 9, 24 (glove) sonya etchison/Shutterstock.com; p. 11 Pete Pahham/Shutterstock.com; p. 13 Comstock Images/Thinkstock.com; pp. 15, 24 (bat) Cheryl Ann Quigley/Shutterstock.com; p. 17 Monkey Business Images/Shutterstock.com; p. 21 tammykayphoto/Shutterstock.com; p. 23 Creatas Images/Thinkstock.com.

Printed in the United States of America

CPSIA compliance information: Batch #CS15GS: For further information contact Gareth Stevens, New York, New York at 1-800-542-2595.

Contents

I love baseball!

It is fun to play.

I wear a leather mitt
on my hand.
This is called a glove.

It helps me catch the ball.

I love throwing
a baseball.

I like to hit the ball.

I use a wooden bat.

I try to hit a home run.

I like to run the bases.

Do you like baseball?

Words to Know

base

bat

glove

Index

24